Barnet Phillips

How to play the game of skat

Barnet Phillips

How to play the game of skat

ISBN/EAN: 9783744736688

Printed in Europe, USA, Canada, Australia, Japan

Cover: Foto ©Lupo / pixelio.de

More available books at **www.hansebooks.com**

HOW TO PLAY

THE GAME

OF

SKAT

BY THE MAJOR.

NEW YORK:

EXCELSIOR PUBLISHING HOUSE.

OF

SKAT.

BY THE MAJ

NEW YORK:

EXCELSIOR PUBLISHING HOUSE.

CONTENTS.

HOW TO PLAY SKAT.

INTRODUCTORY REMARKS.

In the pronunciation of Skat, following the German spelling, there will probably arise an inclination to make the "a" in the word short, whereas it is long, like the "a" in "Father."

The derivation of the term Skat is difficult to determine. In its present form (as played to day) it is about fifteen years old, though the basis of the game is very much older. There are many games of cards where the points are counted as in Skat, and as many others where the Knaves play important parts.

There are technical terms special to every game, which are part and parcel of it, and these exist in Skat. Such particular names had better be retained as far as is possible, but the German names of the cards themselves, we insist should have their English designation allotted to them, otherwise confusion would follow.

In German the Knaves are called "Bauern," or "Jungen," sometimes "Wenzel," as in French they are known as "Valets." As the Knaves play a most important part in game of Skat, we will use the English name for them.

Somewhat of a more difficult task arises if an endeavor were made to anglicise certain terms used in the game, which are the verbs.

In Skat, just as there is in Boston, there exists the faintest element of bluff. A player wishing to play a certain kind of game announces his intention of so doing, and an opponent can declare a better game. In German this is called *gereizt*. As we have a synonymous term in Poker we will designate "gereitzen" as "calling," or "declaring." As an example of this a player may "call" or "declare" a game in diamonds, and another a game in hearts, then as a game in hearts is better than one in diamonds, the one having the game in hearts has "the call," and plays. These terms "calls" and "declaration" are both used in Boston.

Failure to do something proposed in Boston brings with it its penalties, so in Skat then, if a player does not make the game he has called, through bad cards or want of skill, he has to pay a certain number of chips for his failure.

Formerly when Whist was played with ten points,

if a game was scored and won by one side, before the other had made a single point, the winners were paid three times (a Triple) or four times (a Quadruple) whatever the stake might have been. If ten points were scored by partners before five was made by their adversaries, a Double was won.

In Skat there are increasing penalties for non performances governed by the points, as there are increased gains for scoring more than the stipulated points.

It may have been already seen that between Skat and Boston there are certain faint resemblances. 1 fact the general card-player soon becomes aware that there can be no game which is essentially original of its kind. Still in Skat there are many novel features, and for this reason it is particularly interesting.

Such acquaintance then with other games is of assistance to the beginner in Skat, but only up to a certain point.

We are rather inclined to the belief that the difficulty which has arisen so far in acquiring Skat, by means of books, is due to the fact that their authors have insisted too much on the resemblance between Skat and other games. If the same basic laws exist in all games, the rules of cards in Skat and which govern it, whether arbitrary or not, make it an exceptional game.

The player then, who wants to learn **Skat**, must, in a measure, make up his mind that he is acquiring an entirely new game.

Skat is a game into which the elements of skill enters very largely, and though there may be thousands of players, there are but few who are good performers.

This element of skill, which, like Whist, will give the percentage of games to the greatest ability, is, however, more subservient to chance in Skat than in Whist, and this is exactly why Skat is so pleasing.

The unknown quantity is always present, and may overturn the best laid plans, and per contra, what may have seemed a hazardous or reckless "declaration" may be crowned with success.

Skat is a game of combinations, and by that it means that there are several different games incorporated in it, depending of course on the hands. In this respect it resembles Boston. In Boston there is the Little Misery, and Little Misery on the table where no tricks are taken, and Boston, where all the tricks are taken, and nearly these same calls or declarations are to be found in Skat, although the values of the cards differ.

A Boston player will understand this at once, whereas a Whist player will not. Whist never changes its character or main features any more than does

Magna Charta, and though methods of counting may differ, Charles Lamb might sit down to-day, were he alive, and play his rubber with Clay or Cavendish.

To use a Latin saying, we should advise any one who wants to learn Skat to make a *tabula rasa* of his mind, that is to rub off of his mental slate all that he thinks he knows about other games, and to begin afresh.

The true charm of any game, its perfect value, as a recreation, may be judged by the fact as to whether it can be played for the love of the thing. Whist, Euchre, Picket, Cribbage are of this character, and most essentially Skat. It can be played "for love," or for the very smallest stake, because of its inherent excellence.

Let no one believe that Skat cannot be learnt unless by seeing the actual game. The difficulties of acquiring Skat by books have been exaggerated, though somewhat due to the confused methods of explanation. Too much has been taken for granted.

VALUE OF CARDS IN SKAT.—SUITS.—TRUMPS.—MATADORS.—
ETC., ETC., WITH THE EXCEPTIONS.

Skat is a game of three persons. Four persons may make up the party, but only three can play. When there is a fourth, the fourth deals; he is out of the game for the round.

Skat is played with 32 cards, with the four suits, all the cards below the Sevens being excluded, the same as in Euchre. Every game is closed when the ten cards in each hand are played.

Remembering that the game is one of combinations, there are not less than seven (7) different games in Skat, called the "Simple Game," "Tourné," "Solo," "Nullo," "Grando," "Nullo-Open," and "Grando-Open."

There is a family resemblance in the Simple game, Tourné, Solo and Grando, which, when once understood, makes an acquaintance with all of them easy.

The trouble in Skat, which must not be concealed, lies in the exceptions, and these will be fully explained. Such exceptional games arise only when a distinct call is made, the player stating that he intends to make a particular game. At once, when the statement is made, the other players know what is the new character of the game.

DEALING.

The cards must be shuffled, and the first Jack turned determines who shall be dealer. The first cards are given to the left. The player to the right cuts. An exposed card requires a new deal, but the deal does not pass, and the same rule holds in case of a mis-deal.

Each player receives ten cards in all, and there are two cards over, those two cards are known as the Skat.

The method of dealing is to give not more than five cards to each of the three players, and then to put two cards on the table face down, not exposing them, and next to give the other five cards to the players.

Three cards can be given to each player, then the Skat, which is the two cards put on the table, then four more cards to each person, and then three, making ten cards in all to each person.

After the first part of the dealing, for the ten cards are to be given, no matter how the cards are dealt, whether three or five, the Skat must then be put face down on the table. This rule is invariable.

Variations as to whether five cards, or two or three cards, shall be dealt at one time, are permissable, providing not less than two cards, but not more than five, are given at one time.

The order of proposing the game to be tried differs in Skat from all other games. The order is reversed. A deals to B and C. B is known as the first hand, C as the middle, and A as the last hand. A does not ask B what he will play, but A makes the inquiry of C who is to his right. A must have some play or he passes. Should he pass, then C asks B. In case all three have cards which they think can make a game, the one who declares the highest unaertaking, the one incurring the greatest penalty, has the call. If two call the same game, the elder hand has it. The dealer always is the elder hand. If all three pass, and there is no call, there may be a new game dealt. In some cases, what is called Ramps is played, but Ramps does not belong to Skat.

We are now only on the threshold of Skat, and further explanations are in order.

THE SKAT.

In what are called the Simple game, Tourné and Solo, and in Grando, the Skat comes into play. Turned down on the table, it belongs to the player who makes or secures a call. The Skat cannot be looked at under all conditions. Sometimes it makes the trump, and sometimes the points in it are counted for the person who takes it. In certain games it does not figure at all, and remains untouched.

SUITS AND VALUES

In the Simple game, Tourné and Solo :

> Clubs come
> Spades come second,
> Hearts come third,
> Diamonds come last.

As the respective values of these suits must always be born in mind, an example of this can be readily furnished. A Simple game in diamonds gives place to a Simple game in hearts, hearts to spades, and spades to clubs. In Tourné the turning of one card makes the trump, the card being taken from the Skat, but the Knave of clubs, and the other Knaves in the order before mentioned, are always the best trumps, then comes the Ace, Ten, King, Queen, etc., of the trumps turned.

Say some player calls the Simple game, there are no contestants, no one had bid against him, or urged him up higher, then he plays the Simple game. But, as it often happens, some one has declared or called a higher game, as Tourné, then Tourné makes the play. When a play is left to one of the three, the other two become his adversaries. If A plays anything, B and C join together to defeat him, or if it is B who has a call, A and C are his opponents.

POINTS.—GAMES.

In the Simple game, in Tourné, in Solo and in Grando, Skat is a game of points, not of tricks. A, who makes a declare, might take eight tricks, lose two tricks and the game.

In the Simple game, in Tourné, Solo and Grando,

your declaration means that you will make sixty-one points, or more if you can. Failing to make the sixty-one points, scoring sixty points or less, you lose. We repeat purposely the names of these games in Skat, the Simple game, Tourné, Solo and Grando, so as to impress them on the reader's mind, for there are more of these games played than of the others. Nullo, and Grando ouvert, are exceptional calls.

We will now give the character of the points, which present no difficulties.

The Aces count the most, which is eleven. The Tens count ten, the Kings four, the Queens three, and Knaves two. The Nine, the Eight and Seven have no values.

Taking all the count cards, with the Tens, what are they worth?

Four Aces, 11 each........	44 points,
Four Tens, 10 "	40 "
Four Kings, 4 "	16 "
Four Queens, 3 "	12 "
Four Knaves, 2 "	8 "
The total being..........	120 "

The half 120 is 60. To make a Simple game, a Tourné, a Solo or a Grando, and win it, the player

must count in his tricks one (1) point more than sixty,
or sixty-one.   If he only makes sixty points he loses.

Trumps in the game of Skat have their peculiarites,
but present no difficulties.

Remembering the values, first clubs, then spades,
next hearts, and lastly diamonds, the Knave of clubs
is the highest trump, no matter what color may have
been made trumps ;   next is the Knave of spades,
then the Knave of hearts, and lastly comes the Knave
of diamonds.   After the four Knaves, the Ace is the
best card, then come the Ten, next King, Queen, Nine,
Eight and Seven.   As has before been remarked, the
difficulty in Skat is in the exceptions, for in Grando
it is only the four Knaves which are trumps, in the
succession named.   In Nullo there are no trumps
at all.

FOLLOWING SUIT.

In playing, a lead calls for the same suit.   You
must follow suit.   Just as in Whist, if you cannot follow suit you may trump if you wish to, or throw away
any cards at your pleasure.

All the Knaves being trumps, if a heart Solo were
declared, and the Knave of clubs were led, trumps
must be furnished by the other players.

It is not to be expected that even an attentive reader
or an expert card-player can at once seize the main

features of the game, but as good a plan as any will
be to present something like an actual game, which
will explain the character of the Skat and its usages.

PLAYING A GAME.

A, B and C are the performers. A has dealt, and B
declares a game, a Simple game in diamonds. There
is no opposition, and B sets out to make the sixty-one
points, diamonds being trumps. It is a low call,
because a Simple game in hearts would have taken it
away from him by another player, as would have done
a call of spades or clubs.

B, from the fact of his calling, has the privilege of
taking the Skat, which is the two cards not exposed.
He does not show them. Just as in Picket, he incorporates the two cards in his hand, discarding or put-
ting aside two other cards from his own hand, those
which he thinks are of the smallest importance to
him. It may happen that he holds two single Tens, or
only one. He may discard his one, or two Tens, and
stow them away, for whatever points there are in the
Skat belong to him, and add to his count.

Suppose the player B was quite positive of making
fifty-one points, and doubtful about one Ten he held.
'This Ten, if he could save it, would make him exactly
what he wants, which is sixty-one points, and so he
puts it away for safety in his discard.

B, the first player after the dealer, begins his lead. He may have the two best Knaves, Ace, Ten of trumps, the King of his trump suit, which is diamonds. The other trumps may be divided, and all fall to his lead. His opponents, A and C, who follow suit, are doing their best all the time to prevent him counting sixty-one points. When the ten cards in each hand are played out, the count of the cards taken begins. If B has sixty-one points in the cards he has secured, he wins. If he has sixty points he loses.

Beginners, before entering the higher realms of Skat, ought to familiarize themselves with this play, known as the Simple game, for it is the foundation on which Skat has been built. The somewhat confusing addition of three more trumps, viz. : the Knaves, which makes a trump suit of eleven, can be understood. The Skat, and its importance, as giving the person who secures it a sight of twelve cards, is now appreciated.

PENALTIES.

The player, B, has won his Simple game with sixty-one points. He is paid for the call. There are certain fixed charges which accompany all calls Say in this instance a Simple game in diamonds was worth ten chips. A pays B ten chips, as does C. If B had lost he would have paid each of the other players ten, or twenty chips. He may then win or lose twenty points.

B has started out to make his sixty-one points, and can count only somewhere between thirty-one and sixty, then he only pays the penalty, but if he makes only thirty, he is *Schneider*—the translation of which is "cut"—and if he makes no count at all, he is *Schwartz*, or "black," which is equivalent to our white-washed, or the less polite term of "skunked." There are increased penalties for both these unfortunate conditions, as when Whist used to be played when a Double or Triple was lost.

MATADORS.

The possession of the Knaves also add to the value of the hands. Remembering their succession, the Knave of clubs standing first, what are called "Matadors" begins by possessing this particular Knave. A hand having Knave of clubs and Knave of spades, has two Matadors. If the player holds the Knaves of clubs, spades, and hearts, always bearing the succession of suits in hand, he has three Matadors. If he holds them all he has four. But there is more than this. If with the four Knaves he has Ace, King, Queen and Ten, these cards increase the number of his Matadors, so that a hand holding all the Knaves and all the other trumps, would have not less than eleven Matodors in hand. But the absence of the leading

Knave, the one in clubs, prevents the having of Matadors at all. If the best Knave is found in the Skat, of course it belongs to the party who takes it up, and so with two or three Knaves, picking up the missing one in the Skat would make them all Matadors.

Their absence in a player's hand, if he wins his call, his adversaries holding them, makes the Matadors count in his favor. If he loses, and holds Matadors, the having of them increases the penalty. The having, or not having Matadors, by the caller or his opponents, is an important factor, of what a player receives or has to pay out. At the conclusion may be found the full tables of games devised from the rules laid down by the recent Skat Congress held at Altenberg.

PROGRESSION OF THE GAME.

The term Tourné is derived from the French, and means to turn a card, and to play Tourné is to make a bid higher than the Simple game. Solo is higher than Tourné, and Nullo a better call than Solo, and beats a Solo in spades, but Solo in clubs is higher than Nullo. There is no use in asserting that this is an unphilosophical sequence. We have to take the game as it is played. It is the cost of the game in this instance that governs.

Grando comes after a Solo in clubs, then Nullo-

Open. A Grando with, or without Knaves, is the highest call that can be made.

FROM THE LOWEST TO THE HIGHEST GAME.

The game of Skat begins with the lowest call, which is the Simple game, and ends with a Grando with, or without two or more Knaves, which is the highest.

In a tabulated form the games may be seen as follows :

Simple game in Diamonds
" " " Hearts
" " " Spades
" " " Clubs
Tourné " Diamonds
"   " Hearts
"   " Spades
"   " Clubs
Solo   " Diamonds
"   " Hearts
"   " Spades
Nullo
Solo   " Clubs
Nullo-open.

Grando, with or without two or more Jacks.

We do not give the cost of these games here, as we think it would be confusing; but the philosophy of the values will be explained hereafter. By referring to the table of values (page 31) like in Boston, at once the cost of any game can be determined.

WHAT IS TOURNÉ?

The Simple game having been explained, Tourné is played precisely like the Simple game, only the trump is made by the player taking up one of the cards from the Skat, which one card he turns face up on the table. Whatever it is, that is trumps. The person making Tourné the game, may take up either of the two cards he pleases, so that he exposes only one of them ; but he must do so before looking at either of them. Of the two cards he may select either the top or the bottom one, but before looking at them. That card shown is the trump. He must make sixty-one points, or lose. It is played just like the Simple game. The player incorporates the two cards of the Skat into his hand, and discards two. Whatever is in the Skat, or in his discard, belongs to him.

WHAT IS SOLO ?

The player calling Solo declares the trump, and by so doing, he tacitly asserts that he can make his sixty-one points without having recourse to the aid the

Skat might give him. He says a Solo in diamonds, hearts, spades or clubs, whatever he thinks he is strongest in. Though he does not look at the Skat until the game is over, the Skat belongs to him, and any points found there are to his credit. After the ten cards are played in each hand, then only he looks at his Skat.

NULLO.

The player who calls Nullo declares that he will take no trick. There are no trumps here, and the Knaves fall into the usual order of cards, the Ace being highest, then King, Queen, Knave, Ten, Nine, Eight and Seven. If the Nullo player takes a trick he loses. The Skat belongs to him.

NULLO OUVERT OR OPEN

Is a Nullo or a call to make no trick at all, the player exposing all his cards, laying them on the table. It is precisely like "Misery on the table" in Boston. He must take no trick. The Skat is not used.

GRANDO.

This is a declare where the player dispenses with the Skat, as in Solo, and depends on the natural strength of his cards. When the call of Grando is made the player must count his sixty-one. Failing to do this he loses. The four Knaves are the highest trumps, and the only trumps. Aces and Tens of suits are the highest cards, then Kings, Queens, Nines, Eights, as in the other game

RECAPITULATION.

Simple Game.—The player declares a trump, and has the privilege of taking the Skat, and has to make sixty-one points.

Tourné.—The player turns up one of the cards in the Skat, and that card the trump. He must make sixty-one points.

Solo.—Without the Skat the player declares a trump, and must make sixty-one points. He counts the points which may exist in the Skat after the game is closed.

Nullo.—There are no trumps. The Skat is not used. The player must make no tricks. The highest card is the Ace, next King, then Queen, Knave, Ten, Nine, Eight, Seven.

Nullo-Open.—The same as above, only the player exposes his cards.

Grando.—Without the use of the Skat, the four Knaves in their color succession, clubs, spades, hearts and diamonds, being the highest cards, then the Aces and Tens of various suits the next, then the Kings,

Queens, Nines, Eights, Sevens the next, the player must make sixty-one points.

SCHNEIDER AND SCHWARTZ.

A declaration is made in the Simple game, Tourné or Solo. The player who calls it, if he has thirty points or less, loses with "Schneider." He ought to have made sixty-one. The opponents have made then of course ninety, and there is an increased penalty. The rule works both ways. If no points are made at all by the player he is Schwartz, or "black." The same thing happens to the opponents. A player with a strong hand, believing he can make his opponents Schneider, can announce that he is going to make his adversaries "Schneider." In that case, because he announces it there are increased penalties. This is called announcing "Schneider." He can announce, also, that he can make his adversaries "Schwartz."

PLAYS.—ADVANCING THEM AFTER A FIRST DECLARATION.

If in Tourné a Jack be turned up, it may as a fortunate accident, give very much greater strength to a hand, and the player may call Grando Tourné, which is Grando, and is paid as such.

GRANDO WITH THE KNAVES.

Sometimes a player who has been bid up to the highest notch by a Nullo Ouvert—or a Nullo-Open—

will declare Grando without two Matadors, which means that he may hold the Knave of spades and Knave of hearts, or the Knave of spades and diamond. He may win every point, but looking in his Skat he finds there the Knave of clubs. The Knave is his, to his misfortune. He has declared Grando "without two Knaves," but he has found the Knave he does not want, which, he hoped, was in his adversaries hands, in his own Skat, and he loses.

WHEN THERE IS NO CALL, RAMPS.

It sometimes happens that no call is made by the Skat players. In such a case the cards might be thrown down, and new game commenced. By prior arrangement, Ramsch—or Ramps—may be introduced. The three play without recourse to the Skat, and the party taking the most points pays the other players. The four Knaves alone are trumps, and the Aces and Tens, as in Grando, are the highest cards after the Knaves. The person having the most points pays ten to the other players. If two have the same number of points they each pay ten to the person who has the least. If each player has forty points it is a stand off. The Altenberg Skat Congress urges the abandonment of Ramps.

In the Tourné, where it is luck alone which determines the trump, a card may be turned up, which is the only trump the player has. He is certain to lose. If he played he might be made Schneider or Schwartz. In order to save time he may, after the first card is played, at once declare that he cannot make the sixty-one points, and throw up the hand. He pays the smallest penalty the hand calls for. The opponents cannot give up their hands under any circumstances, though they may be certain of defeat.

TO CALL A GAME.

There can be no retrogression. A call cannot go backwards to one of a lesser value. If a call be made in hearts, and driven to spades, the player may call it in clubs; this refers to Solo. In Tourné the turn up regulates the trump, unless a Knave is turned, then the player may call Tourné Grando.

THE PHILOSOPHY OF THE COUNT.

```
Simple games—Diamonds Cost 1
            —Hearts........ 2
            —Spades ....... 3
            —Clubs .... ... 4
```

The way of counting the penalties is increased or diminished with the Matadors held by the player or by his adversaries, or whether there be Schneider or Schwartz made by either the player or his opponents. When Schneider is announced two rates are given. When Schwartz is announced there are four rates. These rates are multiplied by the fixed values made out for the calls. The Matadors being the most changeable of the factors, beginning with one Matador and concluding with eleven, the valuations of game in a tabular form will be found convenient, and such is presented for every possible combination of the game on page 31

HINTS AS TO THE PROPER PLAYING OF SKAT.

The four-handed game with the thirty-two cards, as in Euchre, is well-known. In Skat, which is a three-handed game, the change is somewhat confusing, and added to this are certain combinations, the presence of the Knaves, which are the best trumps. The two cards in the Skat, the Skat being a constant factor, also increases the difficulties.

To play Skat well is an accomplishment which very few possess.

The suits which happen to be short in the person's hand who makes a call are often a matter of surprise. The player of a call has the advantage of making a short suit, by his discard in the Skat. It is his object to have a short suit, so that he can trump the Aces or Tens, or other high cards of his adversaries.

To get the caller between the two opponents is what his adversaries must always endeavor to accomplish It can be seen at once that if the caller of a game is short of a suit, he must trump, otherwise, with their long suit, the adversaries being on both sides of him, will put in all their Aces and Tens, and thus fatten their own points. To prevent this the person who has made the call, is forced to trump, and to trump may weaken his hand.

Strict count must be kept at all stages of the game,

and the caller and his adversaries must know exactly what are the totals in the tricks taken. A good Skat player, when a round is over, always announces the exact number of points he has. In this counting, the player having the Skat, if it has been incorporated in his hand, knows more than his opponents. After four or five plays, good players will be pretty well satisfied as to what is, or what ought to be in the Skat. This knowledged of the points, in every stage of the game, is of use in this way. A player of a call has already scored fifty (50) points, the adversaries have the same numbers. An Ace then, which wins or loses, decides the fate of a game. Even a Knave may make exactly sixty-one. In the same way when a Schneider is possible, and eighty has been made, a Ten or an Ace put in at the right time ends the matter.

Skat is a game which can only be played well after many sittings. The idiosyncracies of various players becomes more prominent in Skat than in any other game. Some are very bold, while other are over timid. It is the element of chance which always predominates.

ADVICE.

We should advise those, who wish to learn the game, to first acquire a knowledge of the Simple game. By playing a half dozen rounds the Simple game can be readily learnt. After that Tourné and Solo ought to present no difficulties, and then Grando, which has the same basis, will be understood. After all, Nullo and Nullo Ouvert, are the only real exceptions.

TABLE OF VALUES.

Life is too short for the Skat player, at least for the American, to count up and figure what are the results.

In the game of Boston, players have a printed card, on which the penalties are indicated. The one found at the conclusion of this brochüre is taken from that in use by the Altenberg Skat Congress, to which august body we acknowledge our indebtedness.

It should be remembered that in some parts of Germany the Simple game is rarely played, and that Tourné is the first game announced. Nevertheless we urge on all players to try the Simple game, as it is the a b c of Skat.

To	Solo.		80	88	96	104	112	88	96	104	112	120	96	104	112	120	128
Clubs.		8	80	88	96	104	112	—	88	96	104	112	120	96	104	112	120	128
Grando.		12	—	—	—	—	—	—	—	—	—	—	—	—	—	—	—
Diamonds.		9	90	99	108	117	126	—	99	108	117	126	135	108	117	126	135	144
Hearts.		10	100	110	120	130	140	—	110	120	130	140	150	120	130	140	150	160
Spades.		11	110	121	132	143	154	—	121	132	143	154	165	132	143	154	165	176
Clubs.		12	120	132	144	156	168	—	132	144	156	168	180	144	156	168	180	192

TABLE OF THE VALUATIONS OF SEAT WHERE THE COST OF EVERY GAME IS PRESENTED.

	Rate of cost	With or without one Matador.					With or without two Matadors.					With or without three Matadors.					With or without four Matadors.				
		Game.	Schneider.	Schneider announced.	Schwarz.	Schwarz announced.	Game.	Schneider.	Schneiner announced.	Schwarz.	Schwarz announced.	Game.	Schneider.	Schneider announced.	Schwarz.	Schwarz announced.	Game.	Schneider.	Schneider announced.	Schwarz.	Schwarz announced.
Simple Diamonds.	1	2	3	4	5	6	3	4	5	6	7	4	5	6	7	8	5	6	7	8	9
Hearts.	2	4	6	8	10	12	6	8	10	12	14	8	10	12	14	16	10	12	14	16	18
Spades.	3	6	9	12	15	18	9	12	15	18	21	12	15	18	21	24	15	18	21	24	27
Clubs.	4	8	12	16	20	24	12	16	20	24	28	16	20	24	28	32	20	24	28	32	36
Tourné Diamonds.	5	10	15	20	25	30	15	20	25	30	35	20	25	30	35	40	25	30	35	40	45
Hearts.	6	12	18	24	30	36	18	24	30	36	42	24	30	36	42	48	30	36	42	48	54
Spades.	7	14	21	28	35	42	21	28	35	42	49	28	35	42	49	56	35	42	49	56	63
Clubs.	8	16	24	32	40	48	24	32	40	48	56	32	40	48	56	64	40	48	56	64	72
Grando.	12	24	36	48	60	72	36	48	60	72	84	48	60	72	84	96	60	72	84	96	108
Diamonds.	9	18	27	36	45	54	27	36	45	54	63	36	45	54	63	72	45	54	63	72	81
Hearts.	10	20	30	40	50	60	30	40	50	60	70	40	50	60	70	80	50	60	70	80	90
Spades.	11	22	33	44	55	66	33	44	55	66	77	44	55	66	77	88	55	66	77	88	99
Clubs.	12	24	36	48	60	72	36	48	60	72	84	48	60	72	84	96	60	72	84	96	108
Nullo.	20																				
Nullo Ouvert.	40																				
Grando.	16	32	48	64	80	96	48	64	80	96	112	64	80	96	112	128	80	96	112	128	144
Grando Ouvert	24					144					168					192					216

	Rate	With or without five Matadors.					With or without six Matadors.					With or without seven Matadors.					With or without eight Matadors.				
Simple Diamonds.	1	6	7	8	9	10	7	8	9	10	11	8	9	10	11	12	9	10	11	12	13
Hearts.	2	12	14	16	18	20	14	16	18	20	22	16	18	20	22	24	18	20	22	24	26
Spades.	3	18	21	24	27	30	21	24	27	30	33	24	27	30	33	36	27	30	33	36	39
Clubs.	4	24	28	32	36	40	28	32	36	40	44	32	36	40	44	48	36	40	44	48	52
Tourné Diamonds.	5	30	35	40	45	50	35	40	45	50	55	40	45	50	55	60	45	50	55	60	65
Hearts.	6	36	42	48	54	60	42	48	54	60	66	48	54	60	66	72	54	60	66	72	78
Spades.	7	42	49	56	63	70	49	56	63	70	77	56	63	70	77	84	63	70	77	84	91
Clubs.	8	48	56	64	72	80	56	64	72	80	88	64	72	80	88	96	72	80	88	96	104
Grando.	12																				
Solo Diamonds.	9	54	63	72	81	90	63	72	81	90	99	72	81	90	99	108	81	90	99	108	117
Hearts.	10	60	70	80	90	100	70	80	90	100	110	80	90	100	110	120	90	100	110	120	130
Spades.	11	66	77	88	99	110	77	88	99	110	121	88	99	110	121	132	99	110	121	132	143
Clubs.	12	72	84	96	108	120	84	96	108	120	132	96	108	120	132	144	108	120	132	144	156

	Rate	With or without nine Matadors.					With or without ten Matadors.					With or without eleven Matadors.				
Simple Diamonds.	1	10	11	12	13	14	11	12	13	14	15	12	13	14	15	16
Hearts.	2	20	22	24	26	28	22	24	26	28	30	24	26	28	30	32
Spades.	3	30	33	36	39	42	33	36	39	42	45	36	39	42	45	48
Clubs.	4	40	44	48	52	56	44	48	52	56	60	48	52	56	60	64
Tourné Diamonds.	5	50	55	60	65	70	55	60	65	70	75	60	65	70	75	80
Hearts.	6	60	66	72	78	84	66	72	78	84	90	72	78	84	90	96
Spades.	7	70	77	84	91	98	77	84	91	98	105	84	91	98	105	112
Clubs.	8	80	88	96	104	112	88	96	104	112	120	96	104	112	120	128
Grando.	12															
Solo Diamonds.	9	90	99	108	117	126	99	108	117	126	135	108	117	126	135	144
Hearts.	10	100	110	120	130	140	110	120	130	140	150	120	130	140	150	160
Spades.	11	110	121	132	143	154	121	132	143	154	165	132	143	154	165	176
Clubs.	12	120	132	144	156	168	132	144	156	168	180	144	156	168	180	192

Popular Books! Popular Books! Popular Books!

HOW TO DRAW AND PAINT.—A complete handbook on the whole art of Drawing and Painting, containing concise instructions in Outline, Light and Shade, Perspective, Sketching from Nature, Figure Drawing, Artistic Anatomy, Landscape, Marine, and Portrait Painting, the principles of colors applied to paintings, etc., etc., with over 100 illustrations.
12 mo., boards, with cloth back......................Price 50 cts.

EXCELSIOR SERIES OF RECITATIONS AND READINGS.—The great demand for new and suitable Readings and Recitations has led to the compilation of these books. Our experience of the past warrants the belief that our efforts will be appreciated by the public. Each number will contain about 176 pages, bound in a beautiful illustrated cover printed in colors.
Nos. 1, 2, 3, and 4 now ready........ ....Price 25 cts. each.

THE COMPLETE DEBATER.—Containing Debates, Outlines of Debates, and Questions for Discussion, to which is added an original and complete debate on Free Trade.
Bound in boards, with cloth back, containing over 200 pages.... ... . Price 50 cts.

WILSON'S BALL-ROOM GUIDE; OR, DANCING SELF-TAUGHT.—The latest and most complete of any publication of its kind out, embracing not only the whole theory and practice of Terpsichorean Art, but full and requisite information for the giving of RECEPTIONS, PARTIES, BALLS, etc., with clear directions for CALLING OUT THE FIGURES OF EVERY DANCE, together with thirty-eight pages of the latest and most fashionable COPYRIGHT music, and containing nearly one hundred figures for the "German."
Bound in illuminated board cover, with cloth back...Price 75 cents.
Bound in illuminated paper cover .... " 50 "

BRUDDER GARDNER'S STUMP SPEECHES AND COMIC LECTURES.—Containing some of the best Hits of the Leading Negro Delineators of the present day, comprising the most Amusing and Side-Splitting Contributions of Oratorical Effusions which has ever been produced to the Public.
Bound in illustrated paper cover...................Price 25 cents.

PAYNE'S BUSINESS LETTER WRITER AND BOOK OF COMMERCIAL FORMS.—Containing specimen letters on all possible business topics, with appropriate answers. Added to this are a great number of forms for Business Papers and Documents, such as Agreements, Leases, Promissory Notes, Mortgages, Bonds, Receipts, and a host of other forms.
Bound in boards, with cloth back.......................Price 50 cts.

DUNBAR'S COMPLETE HANDBOOK OF ETIQUETTE.—This work presents, in a clear and intelligible manner, the whole art and philosophy of Etiquette. Among the contents are : Bodily Deportment, Speak Grammatically, Self-Respect, Pedantry, Social Characters, Traveling, Useful Hints on Conversation, etc., etc.
Bound in boards, cloth back............................Price 50 cts.

BURDETT'S SERIES OF RECITATIONS AND READINGS.—These books contain new and original pieces never before published. The entire series compiled and arranged by the popular and talented humorist, James S. Burdett. No. 1, Dutch Dialect, and No 2, Serio Comic, now ready, to be followed rapidly by No. 3, Negro Dialect; No. 4, Patriotic; No. 5, Dramatic; No. 6, Heroic; No. 7, Shakesperean, etc., etc.
Illustrated paper cover, containing 160 pages ....Price 25 cts.

Excelsior Publishing House, 29 Beekman St., N. Y.

Barkeeper's Manual.—Only professional book of the kind and the recognized standard with New York barkeepers. It gives all plain and fancy mixed drinks, and the popular beverages of all sections. It is designed for hotels, steamers, restaurants, club houses, saloons, and wherever a reliable guide of this kind is required. It also gives chapters on preparation of wines, cordials, liquors, bitters, syrups, aerated summer beverages, artificial champagne, cider, and numerous useful recipes and practical suggestions to the profession.....................50 cts.

Black-Board in the Sunday-School.—A practical guide for Superintendents and Teachers. By FRANK BEARD. With numerous illustrations. Just the thing wanted, giving just the information needed to enable any superintendent or teacher to use the Black-board in the work of the Sunday-School, including instructions for plain and colored drawings and every branch of the subject. Cloth, gold and black stamping....................$1.50

Book of Scrolls and Ornaments.—For Car, Carriage, Fresco, and other Painters. This book is now used in many prominent car shops, and for ornamental work generally. Mr. J. H. Loudolphe gives the best ideas, and his work herein maintains the reputation his work in the shop gave him. It is principally devoted to *flat* ornamentation. The work is a favorite with the profession, and is a storehouse of valuable designs for a great variety of purposes..............$1.00

Book of Alphabets.—For Painters, Draughtsmen, Designers, etc. Including all standard styles and many new and popular ones. Among others, German, French, Old English, etc........50 cts.

Book of Japanese Ornamentation.—A collection of designs adapted to the use of decorators, designers, sign painters, silversmiths, and others. It meets the want created by the prevailing fashion for "Jap," and will be found highly useful for a variety of purposes. The designs are all *practical*, and range from the simplest styles to the most elaborate work. "This collection will be found useful to the sign painter, designer, decorator, and others for whom it is intended."—*Painter's Magazine.* "Deserves study by all painters interested in decoration."—*Hub*....................$2.00

Books of Advertised Wonders.—This is a collection of the secrets, money-making recipes, wonders, and various things advertised by circulars and newspapers to catch curious people. Some are good, some bad, some indifferent. $250 were spent to collect them, and here you have them for 50 cents, with our comments as to the humbugs when they are such. There are enough good things to pay almost any one for the outlay of fifty cents, and many persons will avoid paying much high prices for some by getting this book..............50 cts.

Candy Maker.—A complete guide for making all plain and fancy candies, bonbons, etc. It tells exactly how to boil the sugar or molasses successfully for every kind of candy how to color, flavor, and every operation. This is a good trade in every city, town, and village, and is easily learned. Fresh candies of all fashionable kinds sell readily at immense profits, and will build up a trade in any community now using the factory kinds. Any grocer or baker could add largely to his profit in a small place by introducing a few of these specialties. The book also gives a full line of syrups for soda water, recipes for many popular styles of ice cream, and other information. Illustrated....................50 cts.

Excelsior Publishing House, 29 Beekman St., N. Y.

Art of Training Animals.—A complete guide for amateur or professional trainers, giving all the secrets and mysteries of the craft, and showing how all circus tricks, and all feats of all performing animals—from elephants to fleas—are accomplished. It also has an improved system of horse and colt breaking, breaking and training sporting dogs, care and tuition of song, talking, and performing birds, snake charming, bee taming, and many other things, making a large, handsome volume of over 200 pages and 60 illustrations. It would take a page of this catalogue merely to mention what the book contains. Every farmer and animal-owner will find this book valuable, and every boy who has dogs or other pets will find it a source of endless amusement. One gentleman writes us that his boys have organized quite a circus with their pets, who have been taught amusing and wonderful tricks from our book, and he proposes getting them a little tent. Remember this book at the holidays. It is a good present ....50 cts.

(An edition embracing also The Horseshoer's Manual and Youatt's Treatise on Diseases of the Horse's Foot, in one handsome cloth-bound volume, at $1.00.)

Art of Wood Engraving.—A practical instructor by which any one can learn a good trade. Many young ladies have had gratifying success, and executed very creditable and profitable work after a few months' practice. Profusely illustrated..............25 cts.

Artist's Manual.—A practical guide to Oil and Water-Color Painting, Crayon Drawing, etc. By JAMES BEARD and other eminent artists. Now that so many are taking up art studies, this book meets a want which can be filled by no other single volume. It is very clear, full, and explicit, and teaches the best methods. Mr. Beard is widely and favorably known as an artist and writer, and his book may therefore be relied upon. It gives the able and conscientious aid of an expert, hence is peculiarly helpful. Illustrated...................50 cts.

Bad Memory Made Good, and Good Made Better.—Shows how a wonderful power of memory may be acquired by a simple art, readily, and enables its possessor to achieve feats incomprehensible to those ignorant of the secret. It will be of great assistance to teachers, pupils, and professional men generally. Clergymen and speakers will save much time by its chapter on Speaking without Notes ; students preparing for examination will be greatly aided.............. ..15 cts.

Baker's Manual.—This is a practical instructor in all branches of the business, including American, French, and German styles of work, pastry, cake, and various kinds of bread, biscuit, etc. It gives many novelties whose recipes are sold at high prices, and any baker will find it pay him to get this book. A good idea of the real value of this book is given by the fact that the only similar work, scarcely as large, has been selling to the trade for $5 a copy. Any intelligent cook can make the most palatable and attractive articles with the aid of our plain and simple directions. Special attention is directed to the line of fashionable cakes and pastries. The breadmaking instruction is also very reliable and covers every variety ... .50 cts.

Excelsior Publishing House, 29 Beekman St., N. Y.

German at a Glance.

A new system, on the most simple principles, for Universal Self-Tuition, with English pronunciation of every word. By this system any person can become proficient in the German language in a very short time. It is the most complete and easy method ever published. By Franz Thimm. (Revised Edition.)

Bound in paper cover, - - - **price 25c.**
Bound in boards, with cloth back, - **price 35c.**

French at a Glance.

Uniform and arranged the same as "German at a Glance," being the most thorough and easy system for Self-Tuition. (Revised Edition.)

Bound in paper cover, - - - **price 25c.**
Bound in boards, cloth back, - - **price 35c.**

Spanish at a Glance.

A new system for Self-Tuition, arranged the same as French and German, being the easiest method of acquiring a thorough knowledge of the Spanish language. (Revised Edition.)

Bound in paper cover, - - - **price 25c.**
Bound in boards, cloth back, - - **price 35c.**

Italian at a Glance.

Uniform in size and style with German, French, and Spanish, being the most simple method of learning the Italian language. (Revised Edition.)

Bound in paper cover, - - - **price 25c.**
Bound in boards, cloth back, - - **price 35c.**

Send all orders to

EXCELSIOR PUBLISHING HOUSE,

No. 29 Beekman Street,

NEW YORK.

Painter's Manual.–A complete practical guide to house and sign painting, graining, varnishing, polishing, kalsomining, papering, lettering, staining, gilding, glazing, silvering, analysis of colors, harmony, contrast, philosophy, theory, and practice of color, principles of glass staining, etc. Including a new and valuable treatise on How to Mix Paints. This book is the best general treatise on the painter's trade yet written, and gives the information really wanted. Experienced painters have repeatedly borne witness to its value, and have found hints and helps which they had not happened to learn with years of practice. To the learner the book is simply indispensable.....50 cts.

Phonographic Hand-Book.–For self-instruction in the modern improved system, used by practical reporters in the courts of law and on the newspapers. It unites simplicity with thoroughness, and is the best work for beginners......................... ....25 cts.

Rapid Reckoning.–System of the famous "Lightning Calculator," whose exhibitions seemed almost miraculous; any one can learn and apply; valuable to clerks, bookkeepers, teachers, and business men. "This is not a gift, but a scientific process. * * * It will be of immense advantage in trade, commerce, and science, and revolutionize the tedious mode of addition throughout the world."–*N. Y. Tribune.* It is not a "table-book," but the art of performing arithmetical calculations with almost instantaneous speed by processes fully taught and easily learned by this book.................................25 cts.

Rogues and Rogueries of New York.–Exposes all frauds and swindles of the great cities, from confidence operators to quack doctors, and swindles and humbugs by mail. Nearly 100,000 copies have been sold, and it has broken up many swindles. It is highly interesting, as well as valuable. If you haven't read it, don't fail to do so. Illustrated ....25 cts.

Royal Society Drawing Book.–This book took the prize offered for the *best* by the London Society of Arts. It advances the learner radidly, at the same time making him thorough in all he learns. It is adapted to self-instruction or use in classes. It has the quickest and best methods, clearly presented. Its instructions are exact and always to the point, and so clear that the learner cannot go astray. It is profusely illustrated, covering the whole ground of Free-hand Outline from Outline or from the Flat, Free-hand Outline from Objects or from the Round, and Practice of Free-hand Outline from Solids and Real Objects. If you want to learn drawing understandingly and correctly as well as rapidly, this is the proper guide.................50 cts.

Scene Painting and Painting in Distemper.–This work gives not only full instructions in the preparation of the colors, drawing for scene painters, stage settings, but also useful information regarding stage appliances and effects. It has numerous illustrative diagrams and engravings...$1.00

Secrets Worth Knowing.–A guide to the manufacture of hundreds of useful and salable articles, including patent medicines, perfumery, toilet, and dental articles, and many others easily made at trifling cost; selling readily at large profit. A single article may afford livelihood to person making and introducing to the public; storekeepers, agents, and others can make a line of salable goods and make money in any community.................... ....25 cts.

Excelsior Publishing House, 29 Beekman St., N. Y.

Haney's Fancy Alphabets.—For sign painters. This
work meets a want. It gives the fashionable styles of the day, and original designs of great beauty and utility. Sign painters who want the novelties of New York experts should get this work. It will help you to keep customers and get new ones................. ....50 cts.

Home Recreations; *or, How to Amuse the Young Folks.*—
Designed to afford fresh and agreeable entertainment for juvenile parties, holidays, and the home circle. It will give many pleasant hours and keep young folks out of mischief, and make them find employment, in their home circle contentedly. Parents, get a copy by all means Illustrated........... .... 25 cts.

Horse-Shoer's Manual.—Includes preparation of foot,
choice of shoes and their preparation, fitting, filing, nails and nailing, shoeing with leather, cutting, removing, etc. Also, Youatt's Treatise on Diseases of Horses' Feet. Bonner's famous horse, Dexter, owed much of his value to good shoeing, and with all horses it is of grave importance. This book should be in the hands of every professional horse-shoer, and every horse-owner............................ ....25 cts.

Houdin the Conjurer.—This life of the famous French
Conjurer is full of interesting adventures, "more fascinating than fiction." Illustrated with numerous engravings ....50 cts.

How I Became a Ventriloquist.—Describing the methods
by which the author acquired the amusing art, and also his diverting experience therewith..10 cts.

How to Make Up for the Stage.—A practical illustrated
guide for amateur theatricals, charades, tableaux, etc. This is invaluable to any one getting up, or participating in, any of these entertainments .... 15 cts.

Humors of Ventriloquism.—Full of the most entertain-
ing and laughable scenes, etc..10 cts.

Hunters and Trappers' Practical Guide.—This little
book has immense sale, and gives satisfaction every time. It is a practical guide to gunning and rifle shooting, tells how to choose arms and ammunition, about different kinds of game, making and using traps, snares, and nets, baits and baiting trailing game, preserving, dressing, tanning, and dyeing skins and furs; season for trapping, hints to trappers, fire hunting, pigeon catching, camping out; sporting vocabulary, recipes for sportsmen, secret of successful fishing. It has more information than books costing $1 to $2, and must not be confounded with any catchpenny. It has fifty engravings.............. .....20 cts.

Impromptu Speaker.—This is not a collection of set
speeches, but guides the speaker in making his own. To point out the requirements of all ordinary occasions of impromptu speech-making, and to afford such aid as may be useful, are the aims of this little treatise. While avoiding formal rules and elaborate disquisitions, care will be taken to show clearly the things to avoid, as well as the things to strive for, in both the matter and the manner of the speech, and the particular points of etiquette to be observed......................25 cts.

Second Sight.—A guide to performing this famous feat as practiced by Heller and other Conjurers, adapted to parlor or school exhibitions, with a *new* method of performing never before published, far more easy of performance and bewildering in its effect upon an audience...15 cts.

Self Cure of Debility.—*Including Consumption, Dyspepsia, Nervousness, etc.* Advertises no doctor or medicine, but gives full and plain instructions for self cure by simple means within reach of all, which will cost *nothing*, and are the surest, safe, and quickest methods of cure. Dangers of advertised modes of treatment, quack nostrums, etc., are pointed out. It will do more than anything else to break up quackery, for it tells the truth, and quackery thrives on falsehood ....75 cts.

Self Cure of Liquor and Opium Habits.—This book exposes dangers and fallacies of advertised modes of treatment and quack nostrums, and gives the best and most successful treatment known. This book gives recipes for preparations which can be given in tea, coffee, or other fluid unknown to the drinker, to cure the liquor habit. These preparations are advertised and sold at high prices..75 cts.

Self Cure of Stammering.—The most approved and successful methods of Self-Treatment, with exposures of empirical and dangerous devices. By aid of this book many sufferers have overcome embarrassing impediments, and its information is the stock in trade of several "schools" and "professors," who are doing a lucrative busi ness...25 cts.

Sign, Carriage, and Decorative Painting.—This book is the combined work of several prominent painters, and is full of valuable points upon the several branches of the trade, very complete. It includes Fresco and Car painting, and other useful matters. ... 50 cts.

Sign Writing and Glass Embossing.—This standard work, so widely and favorably known, is now issued in new edition, with newly engraved illustrations, and at a greatly reduced price. This work is too well known to the trade to need eulogy at our hands. It has been long regarded as a standard work and invaluable to every one interested in its line..75 cts.

Slow Horses Made Fast, *and Fast Horses Made Faster.* —System of increasing speed practised by the most famous and successful horsemen. Endorsed by Robert Bonner, Esq. Illustrated, 50 cts.

Sketching from Nature in Pencil and Water Colors, —This is an excellent work for young art students ; full of practical information, which they will find clearly presented. Illustrated. 50 cts.

Snares of New York.—The most complete exposure of the perils and pitfalls of this city, the clever devices of wily men and women to entrap the innocent or the stranger, and the traps of swindledom high and low. A mammoth double-column volume of nearly 200 pages, profusely illustrated..................................50 cts.

Excelsior Publishing House, 29 Beekman St., N. Y.

Comicalities by Orpheus C. Kerr.—A capital work by this very popular American humorist. Containing 150 comic engravings...25 cts.

Common Sense Cook Book.—A large and excellent collection of approved cooking and domestic recipes................25 cts.

Infant Star Speaker.—A collection of choicest pieces for little speakers, adapted to different styles and abilities. A valuable feature of this book is the instruction on training and managing the little speakers, and how to make the most effective appearance at school receptions and exhibitions.................................25 cts.

Joe Green's Trip to New York.—A highly diverting account of a stranger's amusing haps and mishaps in the metropolis. Illustrated...10 cts.

Lessons in Horse Judging.—A practical guide for dealers and buyers, by which any intelligent person may become a good judge of horses..50 cts.

Manual of Hair Ornaments.—For jewelry or souvenirs. A guide for a tasteful recreation for leisure hours, and a source of profitable employment for jewelers and others. This book gives full directions whereby any one can acquire the art. The book is illustrated with over eighty explanatory engravings and beautiful designs for work...50 cts.

Marine and Landscape Painting in Oil.—A practical guide, fully illustrated...50 cts.

Marine and Landscape Painting in Water-Colors.—A practical guide, fully illustrated.................................50 cts.

Marvels and Mysteries of Detective Adventure.—A collection of thrilling and interesting stories of the detectives. Illustrated...25 cts.

Mind Reading.—A practical explanation of the curious phenomena exhibited by "Brown, the Mind Reader," enabling any one to perform the experiments. Illustrated...................15 cts.

Nightside of New York.—This book is a vivid and truthful portrayal of the great city after the gas is lighted. It presents high and low life as they actually are; the fashionable life and life in the slums. It does not seek sensationalism, nor to draw on fancy for its matter. "Truth is stranger than fiction." Illustrated..........25 cts.

Practical Mesmerist, The.—A plain and practical illustrated self-instructor in Curative and Scientific Mesmerism, teaching how the reader may acquire and practice the art; how to detect disease, to retard or accelerate the circulation of blood, to cure headache, rheumatism, tic doloreau, mental disorders, paralysis, spinal disease complaints of lung, liver, heart, and stomach, etc.; introvision, or power of looking into the body, clairvoyance, mesmerized water, to make a person subject to your will or command, and many curious experiments. Third edition, with much important additional matter, with numerous illustrations...25 cts.

Excelsior Publishing House, 29 Beekman St., N. Y.

Carpenter's Manual.—Instructs in the use of tools and the various operations of the trade, including drawing for carpenters, forms of contracts, specifications, etc., with plain instructions for beginners, and full glossary of terms used in the trade. Also gives plans and specifications for building a number of frame houses. Illustrated..50 cts.

Detective's Club.—A most interesting book of detective life and adventure. Curious, amusing, and thrilling. Large illustrated volume..25 cts.

Diseases of Dogs.—Their pathology, diagnosis, and treatment; to which is added a complete dictionary of canine materia medica. A practical guide for every dog owner. Tells how to prevent as well as to cure diseases, and gives much information on care and management of dogs. If you have a valuable sporting or watch dog, or a pet dog of any kind, you should get this book for its valuable suggestions on care of dogs, and for handy reference in any emergency. It is thoroughly reliable, and simple and explicit in its language. 25 cts.

Dog Training.—Chapters on dog training from the "Art of Training Animals." The following briefly gives an idea of its contents: Watch dogs, their selection and value, shepherd's dogs, different kinds and their respective merits and defects, their rearing and training. Varieties and merits of sporting dogs; preliminary training, lessons in the field; water dogs. *Performing Dogs*—Simple tricks and training, to teach him his name, to leap, to walk erect, to dance, to jump rope, to sit and lie down at command, to beg, to give his paw, to sneeze, to speak for it, to fetch and carry, to bring you his tail in his mouth, to stand on a ball and roll it up and down a plank, to walk on stilts, to go up and down a ladder, to stand on his head, and walk on fore-legs, to "sing," lump of sugar trick, to feign death..........25 cts.

Dyer and Scourer.—A complete practical guide, designed especially for the use of job dyers. It includes dyeing silk, stuff, or mixed goods, cotton, raw wool scouring, scouring for job dyers, and job dyeing in all its branches..50 cts.

Employment Seeker's Guide.—Gives advantages and objections of different trades and professions; how to succeed in business; how to get good situations, new openings, and much valuable practical information. Boys and young men will get useful hints from its pages that may assist them throughout their business career. Parents would find it a good book, interesting, as well as helpful, to place in the hands of sons or daughters, as the employments of women are also treated.. 25 cts.

Fun Everlasting.—A large collection of choice humorous stories, jests, puns, witticisms, etc., which will afford hearty laughter, the whole illustrated by numerous comic engravings. You can invest a dime with certainty of being well pleased, to say nothing of giving your whole family something to amuse them into the bargain. It is one of the best selling funny books, and it pleases every time ..10 cts

Furniture and Cabinet Finisher.—A guide to polishing, staining, dyeing, and other preparations of hard and soft woods, including the various imitations of costly woods, and a multitude of trade recipes, and secrets of the trade .... 50 cts.

Soap-Maker's Manual.

—Plain and practical guide for the manufacture of plain and fancy soaps, washing fluids, medicinal soaps, toilet preparations, shaving soaps and creams, soap powders, etc , for families and manufacturers. Has best American, English, French, and German formulas. Any family in the country can make good soap at trifling cost. ....25 cts.

Spirit Mysteries Exposed.

—A complete exposition of all the marvelous feats of the "spirit rappers" and "mediums," Daven-ports, Hume, etc., so fully laid bare that any one can perform. The young folks can astonish and amuse their companions and friends by exhibitions of these mysterious doings, doing the wonders seen at private and public seances. Illustrated......................15 cts.

Standard Sign Writer, The.

—This book is very generally recognized as the *standard* work on the subject. Its instructions are clear, precise, and practical, and cover just the ground desired by most of the profession It is divided into two parts, the first giving detailed instructions for the different styles of lettering according to the prac-tices most approved by the best practical sign-writers. The second part consists of a variety of large engraved plates, designed especially for this work, and giving some of the best styles of lettering, model alphabets, designs for signs, and other things of interest to the profes-sion $2.00

Standard Scroll Book, The.

—This is a collection of upward of *two hundred* designs suitable for painters, jewelers, designers, deco-rators, draughtsmen, and almost every branch requiring ornamental scroll work Prominent features in this book are the *Shaded scrolls* and the designs for *Signs, Wagons,* and *Omnibuses*.....................$1.00

Standard Irish Readings.

—Gives choicest selections in prose and verse, many rare ones, suited to recitation or public reading. While specially interesting to Irish people, many of the pieces are well adapted to general use, being very fine...........................25 cts.

Taxidermist's Manual.

—This is the only complete and practical work giving full and plain instructions for collecting, pre-paring, preserving, stuffing, and mounting all birds, animals, and in-sects ....50 cts.

Tricks on Travelers.

—A little work exposing frauds practised on travelers, and other information useful to strangers in great cities, Illustrated ....15 cts.

Uncle Si's Black Jokes.

—This is one of the funniest books you ever saw. It is quaint and curious, and real darkey humor. Illustrated ....10 cts.

Use of Colors.

—A valuable treatise on the properties of different pigments and their suitableness to uses of artists and students. Full of useful information ....25cts.

Watchmakers and Jewelers' Manual.

—Gives latest and most approved secrets of the trade, embracing watch and clock cleaning and repairing, tempering in all its grades, making tools, com-pounding metals, alloys, plating, etc., with plain instructions for beginners. Greatly enlarged edition .... 50 cts.

Excelsior Publishing House, 29 Beekman St., N. Y,

New and Popular Books sent Free of Postage at Prices Annexed.

Brudder Gardner's Stump Speeches and Comic Lectures.

—Containing some of the best Hits of the Leading Negro Delineators of the present day, comprising the most Amusing and Side-Splitting Contributions of Oratorical Effusions which has ever been produced to the Public. Bound in illustrated paper cover..25 cts.

Progressive Euchre and How to Play It.

—Being also a complete guide to the various ways of playing "Euchre," by J. B. In an elegant artistic cover...10 cts.

German at a Glance.

—A new system, on the most simple principles, for Universal Self-Tuition, with English pronunciation of every word. By this system any person can become proficient in the German language in a very short time. It is the most complete and easy method ever published. By Franz Thimm. Revised Edition. Bound in paper cover..25 cts.
Bound in boards, with cloth back.......................... 35 cts.

French at a Glance.

—Uniform and arranged the same as "German at a Glance." Revised Edition. Bound in paper cover..25 cts.
Bound in boards, cloth back ....35 cts.

Spanish at a Glance.

—A new system for Self-Tuition, arranged the same as French and German, Revised Edition. Bound in paper cover ....25 cts.
Bound in boards, cloth back ....35 cts.

Italian at a Glance.

—Uniform in size and style with German, French, and Spanish. Revised Edition. Bound in paper cover..25 cts.
Bound in boards, cloth back....................................35 cts.

Byrne's Lumber and Log Book, Ready-Reckoner and Price Book.

—By Oliver Byrne, Civil, Military and Mechanical Engineer. "Byrne's Ready-Reckoner" is the most concise, complete, and correct work ever issued. Boards................35 cts.

Madame Zadkiel's Perfect Fortune Teller.

—Containing Answers, Astragalomancy, Augury by Dice, Calendar of Fate, Cauls, Candle Omens, Charm of the Rose, etc., etc. With illustrations and a double-page chart printed in colors. 156 pages, 16mo. Illuminated board cover............. ....35 cts.

Napoleon's Oraculum; or, Book of Fate.

—Including the true Interpretation of Dreams, Visions, and Omens of the Wedding Day. By the Countess of Blessington. The Egyptian Circle; or, Ancient Wheel of Fortune. Illustrated, etc., etc. 48 pages, 16mo, paper cover..10 cts.

Madame De Stael's Dream Book and Fortune Teller.

—With Illustrated Charts. 48 pages, 16mo, paper cover.........10 cts.

EXCELSIOR PUBLISHING HOUSE, 29 & 31 Beekman St., New York, N.Y.
P. O. Box 1144.

www.ingramcontent.com/pod-product-compliance
Lightning Source LLC
Chambersburg PA
CBHW031814090426
42739CB00008B/1272